TURNED ON

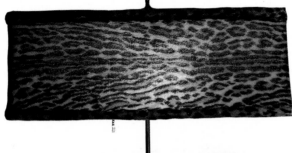

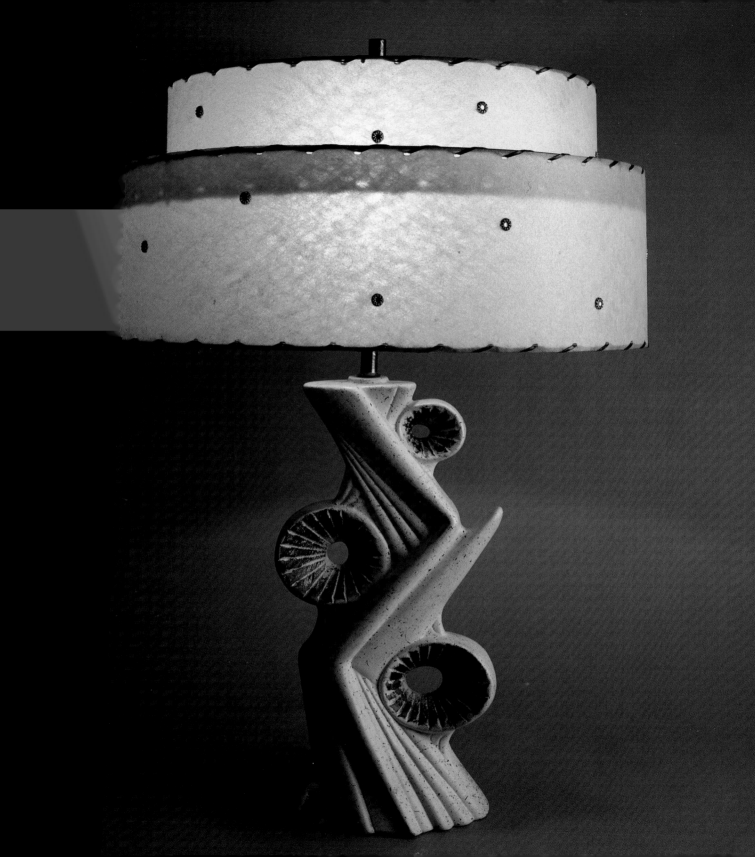

TURNED ON

Decorative Lamps of the 'Fifties

LELAND & CRYSTAL PAYTON

PHOTOGRAPHS BY LELAND PAYTON

ABBEVILLE PRESS · PUBLISHERS · NEW YORK

For Strader
and Ross Daniels Payton,
the lights of our lives.

Editor: Walton Rawls
Designer: Julie Rauer
Production Supervisor: Hope Koturo

Library of Congress Cataloging-in-Publication Data

Payton, Leland.
Turned on : decorative lamps of the fifties / Leland & Crystal Payton ; photographs by Leland Payton.
p.   cm.
ISBN 0-89659-916-7 : $19.95
1. Electric lamps—United States—Themes, motives. 2. Decoration and ornament—United States—
History—20th century. 3. Kitsch—United States.   I. Payton, Crystal.   II. Title.
NK6196.P39   1989
749'.63—dc20   89-36268
                                                                                      CIP

CONTENTS

Shocking
LAMPS

In the 1920s, classic modernists maintained that good design would change the world. Unfortunately, human history has subsequently failed to validate this thesis. Good taste, the idea that surrounding oneself with objects of certain austere shapes and colors can make one a better person, seems to be an idea whose time has either bypassed us or not yet come. Today the spice of stylistic choice in much contemporary design is, of course, hardly distinguishable from what has been thought of as bad taste.

Interest in badly designed objects seems to have begun as an evil fascination for European intellectuals (notably in the writings on kitsch of Gillo Dorfles and Jacques Sternberg), but with the gradual development of Pop Art sensibilities in America this interest has grown into outright love. Remember the phrases "so bad it's good" and "guilty pleasures"?—they seem to indicate that try as we might, our hearts and sense of humor remain at variance with our heads and strict modernist ethics. Postmodernism, whatever that term now encompasses, definitely confirms that kitsch objects are not to be automatically thrown out with the trash. In an era that increasingly embraces the worst in design, popular domestic lighting is a conspicuously neglected subject in the literature.

This book, therefore, can best be appreciated as a quest for understanding and enjoyment of the ugly lamp. Permit us then to shed some light on an object with what might be regarded as a limitless capacity to meld absurd sculpture, incompatible color, and flagrant disregard for function. Unrestrained by design traditions and untouched by architectural principles, the electric lamp possibly exceeds all other domestic artifacts in its potential for being awful.

This bulb-bearing beauty is not unique; we've seen another version that has two of these rope, wood, and grass girls under a palm tree.

Inscrutable Eastern potentate of the Dumont. Oriental motifs in lighting were common and popular.

As a trip to any art museum will confirm, the birth of bad is hard to pinpoint, for questionable taste and wretched excess belong to the ages. The sands of time have doubtless spared us many antique masterpieces of dysfunction and overdone ornamentation, but from the Renaissance on, trixies, pixies, and nubile Nubians have been pressed into service to support varying light sources for the rich and famous. Of late, political enlightenment and mass production have made it possible for a great many more to enjoy such treasures. A tricky point indeed is to regularly distinguish between previously owned lamps auctioned at Sotheby's and secondhand materials offered at the Ventura swap meet. Melt value of raw material and age seem often to be the main differences, besides selling price.

Mermaids mount the base of this artist-signed ("Colette") ceramic lamp.

As in Reaganomics, there is in esthetics a "trickle down" theory of art. Without totally disputing the widely held concept that stylistic innovation begins at the top and gradually works its way down to the bottom of society, we believe this study of popular lamps reveals some unexpected and surprising variations on the theme. A great many American ceramic lamps produced in the 1950s definitely show the strong influence of French Art Moderne styling of the 1920s and 1930s. However, the simplification necessitated by mass production in the 1950s produced forms that have, in turn, inspired serious artists from the 1960s on. Many stylistic aspects of mass-market debasement are, in fact, observable today in high art and fashion. The "trickle down" phenomenon is, in fact, an ebb and flow in exchanging stylistic forms.

Not all shocking lamps are worthy of contemplation. As with most industrial artifacts, the average electric lamp is not desirably bad enough. Most are just outright ugly

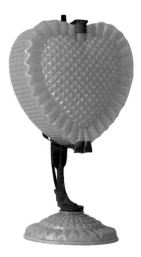

A sweetheart of a boudoir lamp, this Depression-glass ruffled heart came as a set with another table lamp and a third glowing heart to hang from the bed's headboard.

No. 522/23-16"
Height overall, 21½"

No. 771/0280-16"
Height overall, 23"

No. 781/6263-18"
Height overall, 22"

No. 6a18/__
Height overall

No. 552/421-
Height overall

No. 5___-
Final cover to us

Patriotic, nautical, antiquarian, and moderne lamps are available for the style-conscious 1963 housewife/decorator—even through the Top Value Stamps catalog.

Offered in the 1926 catalog of the Jefferson Glass Company of Follansbee, West Virginia, these lamps ". . . when lighted, are a beautiful revelation of what can be accomplished in artistic lighting when lamps . . . are placed in a room."

or terminally pretentious. Our tropism tends toward fixtures that transcend taste and skewer the tender niceties of drab drawing-room esthetics. They stuck out then, and you can spot them today across a crowded sec-ondhand store. Take one home. Clean it up (the best are always glazed with nicotine). Rewire it if necessary, and plug it in. Invite your family or friends to watch you turn the thing on. You will all smile and feel bolder, freer. You are Turned On.

When only the "best" will do, the thrifty, stamp-pasting consumer must surrender 8³⁄₅ books of Top Value stamps for No. 12, the most expensive lamp on the page: the "Hall Bristol Table Lamp with complete hand decoration and tapered neck flowing into a smart global shaping."

SHOW TIME...

Airbrushed ceramic mallards rivaled black panthers as popular '50s TV lamps.

Flamingo TV lamps are uncommon and highly sought after. This is by Lane and Co., Van Nuys, Cal., dated 1957.

Postwar affluence brought on a taste for opulence, and a liberal splashing of gold decoration graced many a lamp.

A plastic prom queen from the 1950s. The ruffles and flounces of her sweeping skirt (which also conceals a small light) are echoed in the full and frilly shade.

Motorized hula girl lamps from the 1940s and early '50. Turn the switch and the bulb glows; turn it again and the girl's hips sway in a mechanical hula dance.

The allure of the South Pacific was a favorite design theme, and grass-skirted girls graced all kinds of lamps, from the boudoir to the living-room table. A colored bulb behind the screen adds a romantic glow.

Although most '50s TV lamps were made of high-glaze ceramic, some (like this dying stag) were made of painted plaster, a lingering statement of the 19th-century chalkware animal folk tradition.

A '50s TV lamp continues the late Deco themes of sleekness, speed, and grace in lamp design.

Stylized Art Deco horses rear up on the black glass base of this unmarked 1930s lamp.

Let There Be
LIGHT

We need light. We extol it in song and liturgy. It comforts us. It protects us. It defines territory. But how do we handle it? For millennia we were constrained by its most common form: fire (inherently hot, ever threatening to burn fingers and reduce shelters to ashes). To provide light efficiently, fire had to be contained and its fuel source resupplied on a continuous basis—formerly through a bulbous oil receptacle in a lamp's base or a wick embedded in a long, waxy candle.

Although knowledge of electricity and many of its properties had been around for centuries, its practical application, until the late nineteenth century, had been limited. Most early experiments had focused on the relationship of electricity and magnetism or on efforts to store electricity. In the early nineteenth century, Sir Humphry Davy, an English chemist, while experimenting with the physical properties of electricity, found that this mysterious force could heat thin strips of metal to a point where they glowed brightly. Platinum, he discovered, did not oxidize as rapidly as other metals and could be brought to a white heat and give off light for some time before burning up.

This primitive forerunner of the incandescent lamp spurred scientists and inventors on both sides of the Atlantic into action. In 1841 the British government granted the first patent on an incandescent lamp to Frederick De Moleyns. Continuing experiments throughout the nineteenth century produced numerous variations on this lamp—usually a glass bulb enclosing a carbonized element in a vacuum, and using direct current as a power source. None of these, however, was commercially practical: they had short lives, were expensive to operate, and were unreliable.

Although the bulb designed by Edison contained the essential elements of the modern incandescent bulb, many modifications and incremental improvements have followed: tungsten filaments, alternating current, standardized bases and bulb sizes, increased wattages, frosted and colored glass.

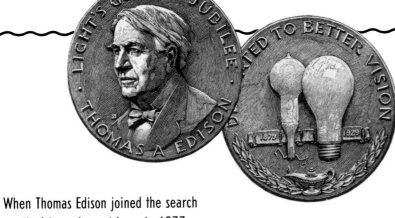

When Thomas Edison joined the search for a practical incandescent lamp in 1877, he was already a well-established inventor with an elaborate laboratory in Menlo Park, New Jersey, and a large staff of assistants and workmen. For two years he worked on the problem, attacking it from all sides—the design of the bulb, the design of the electric circuits, the search for the ideal filament. On October 21, 1879, he first demonstrated his "high resistance carbon lamp." To the surprise and delight of his assistants (some of whom made bets on how long the lamp would stay lit), it burned steadily for nearly two days. On December 21, 1879, he announced his invention to the public in a front-page article in the *New York Herald.* Several scientists called the invention a fake, but the stocks of gas companies dropped in value while the Edison Electric Light Company soared to $3,500 a share.

Being a businessman as well as an inventor, Edison realized that his remarkable electric light bulbs would be of little use unless households had access to a power sup-

ply. In 1882 he started up the Pearl Street Station in New York City, the first power plant designed to supply electricity to consumers.

The earliest light bulbs were dim, inefficient, and gave off a yellow-orange light of about 25 watts. If used for ambient illumination they were most often in ceiling fixtures shaded by frosted or etched glass, or frequently not covered at all. The new electric wiring was often simply pulled through the

General Electric celebrated the Golden Jubilee of Edison's first light bulb patent in October 1929. It was an extravagant celebration for "the father of this age of light," with a 19-page section in *The Saturday Evening Post,* elaborate window displays, and a live radio broadcast from Dearborn, Michigan, where Henry Ford had spared no expense in setting the stage for this ceremonial Jubilee. (*Light* magazine, 1929, National Lamp Works of General Electric Company)

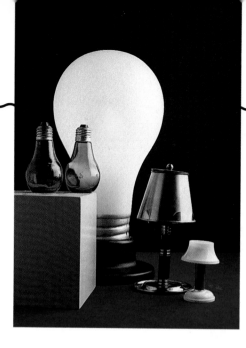

The electric light bulb and the table lamp have lent their familiar forms to salt and pepper shakers, cigarette holders, and even lamps shaped like incandescent bulbs.

walls inside pipes formerly used to deliver gas to lighting fixtures. With the same efficiency, electric bulbs were often hooked up inside the flowered globes of decorative Victorian oil lamps.

As electric power became more reliable and widespread, lamps began to be designed specifically with bulbs and wiring incorporated. Louis Comfort Tiffany (who with Edison designed the fittings for New York's Lyceum, the first electrically lit theater) first presented his elaborate leaded-glass lamps to the public in Chicago in 1893. The domestic lamp quickly assumed a statuary role—one that projected personality, that of the maker certainly, but even more that of the owner and the interior it lighted.

In the twentieth-century house, lamps were almost unique in their decorative

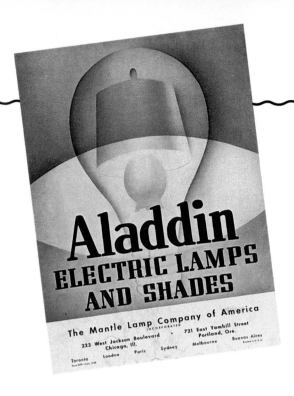

potential. Their function remained simple: conceal the wiring and hold up the bulb and shade. For the first time, the "flame," the light, did not have to go up. The new electric bulbs could be pointed down and sideways as well as up. Such flexibility allowed for all previous lighting designs and added infinitely more. The forms were subject to wild imaginings and flights of fancy, not to mention the general sentimental, flowery, classical, snobbish (and other) expressions of human identity unleashed by the newly created Age of Abundance.

The simplicity of the technology made lamp and shade manufacturing a growth business. Many companies produced only shades—from Steuben Art Glass to painted parchment beauties turned out by hundreds of "studios" across the country. Others manufactured lamp bases, sans shades. Few had the complete facilities of Tiffany Studios. Except for "Pat. Pending" and the more recent "Underwriters Laboratories, Inc.," many mass-market lamps bear no markings. What may have been paper or metal labels have long since disappeared, like many of the companies that made the lamps.

Conferring specialness on ordinary household objects with minimal investment is a dominant mass-market force as vital today as it was in great-grandmother's day. An intricate base of cast pot metal, a splash of gilt, a decal of pink lilies, perhaps a lampshade with a fringe, and voilà!, the sharp manufacturer has turned a plain, wired vase into a special and pricey object. Most of the lamps we present have a sincerity and personality that separates them from such intentions. Indeed ceramic figural lamps, often made in California, might be viewed as Populuxe Staffordshire. The best of the fifties table lamps are certainly not of this earth.

By the 1930s, modernist lighting styles were relegated primarily to architectural settings and used in commercial or office interiors. "It was our aim to produce Lighting Units to conform with modern ideas and buildings," stated the Kopp Glass catalog of 1938.

"... for it designates that which is different in interior lighting. It designates a line which brings you profit in all classes, a line which embodies art of the French, English, Moorish, Old Spanish and the futurist."

A light for every place, and every place bathed in light. Widespread availability of cheap electricity made beating back the darkness a possibility for every home.

For reading with a table lamp, maintain the distances shown above. Use a 50-100-150-watt three-way bulb (set at 150 watts) or a plain 150, plus a diffusing bowl, or a 150-watt white indirect light without the bowl.

Over-all height of lamp may be from 25 to 30 inches. Top of diffusing bowl should be 8 to 9 inches across. Minimum diameter for bottom of shade is 16 inches.

The Aladdin Electric Lamp Company was one of the few companies that produced both lamps and shades. Their "Whip-O-Lite" shades ("The Parchment Eternal") were trademarked and added "in no small measure to their class and distinction."

Cautionary ads warned of the need for the "proper" amount and placement of lighting in the home. "Light conditioning your home" became a matter of exact measurement of distances, angles, and wattages, all to prevent the horrors of eyestrain.

The sun "His only rival" is General Electric's proud boast about the Edison Mazda Lamp. A surprising number of early (before the era of planned obsolescence) light bulbs still work.

SAVE THAT TWINKLE!

Eyestrain starts when children begin to use their eyes. That's the time you need to pay attention. Help their eyes develop normally— (1) by having their eyes examined regularly, (2) by providing lighting that helps them see safely.

The first step in securing good lighting is to use high quality lamp bulbs, the kind that don't waste electricity and that STAY BRIGHTER LONGER. Insist on MAZDA lamps made by General Electric.

Why take the chance of getting 30% less light for your money and of cheating your eyesight, by using inferior substitutes? The mark ⓖ on the end of the bulb is sure protection against substitution. Look for it when you buy lamp bulbs.

GENERAL ⓖ ELECTRIC

"Skimpy Wiring"— skeleton in many dream-home closets!

Sad, but true! Skimpy Wiring lurks in 80% of American homes — including brand new and remodeled houses!

He blows fuses, slows down appliances, dims lights, makes TV pictures shrink. And when you want to add new appliances — often you *can't*. Skimpy Wiring's weak, undersized wires and overloaded circuits just won't let you!

Keep this electrical nightmare out of your dream home! See your electrical contractor or power company about full HOUSEPOWER with *copper* wiring!

Get your FREE booklet —"The ABC of Home Wiring." Write Kennecott Copper Corporation, 161 East 42nd Street, Dept. A-117, Box 238, New York 46, N. Y.

Kennecott Copper Corporation

Fabricating Subsidiaries: Chase Brass & Copper Co. · Kennecott Wire & Cable Co.

THE AMERICAN HOME, NOVEMBER, 1957

Kennecott Copper Corporation's "Skimpy Wiring" was an electrical pest that could subvert even the best-thought-out lighting design, simply by not delivering the proper amount of power. He "makes lights flicker, appliances slow down, TV pictures 'wince' and shrink in size." Clearly, there was more to think about in home lighting than just the style of the lamp.

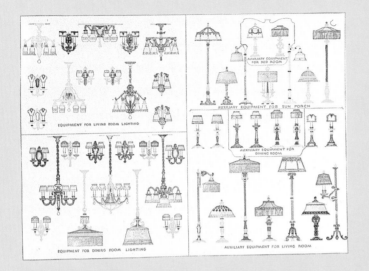

Lovely Living

The Home Lighting Primer, 1924, outlines rules for a "Home Lighting Essay Contest" for Canadian and American schoolchildren. It was an elaborate contest intended to instruct the young on the proper number and placement of lamps to chase away "Gloom" and "Glare."

Pictures of light fixtures were cut out and applied to line drawings of different rooms to show how the contestant would place lamps for correct lighting and proper shading.

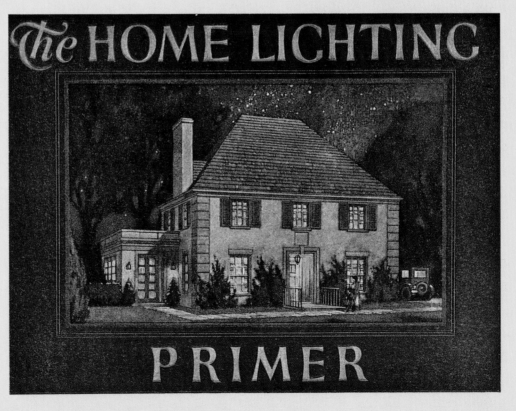

The HOME LICHTING

PRIMER

To Clothe a
NAKED BULB

Popular decorative lighting, as opposed to art lighting, may march to its own drummer, but it can occasionally hum the tunes of high style. Certainly the coincidence that domestic electric lighting became a reality when Art Nouveau was in flower cannot be underestimated. Women and plants have been the inspiration for electric-lamp design since the 1890 to 1910 productions of René Lalique, Emile Gallé, Daum Frères, and, of course, Louis Comfort Tiffany. As well as continuing to recognize the appropriateness of feminine themes for lamps, much of Art Nouveau lighting was really illuminated sculpture. Tiffany and Gallé made *self-illuminated* glass sculpture: lamps not to read by but art to look at.

Even before the electric lamp arrived, oil and gas lighting fixtures were by no means things of functional beauty. "Leave no surface unadorned" was the motto of Victorian lamp-makers as well as Victorian architects. And the urge to ornament was sometimes disastrous since silk and paper shades (remarkably like today's) were not always safely distanced from the open flames of oil lamps. The rationale for permitting a fashionable fire hazard in the house was a reduction in eyestrain, and there were numerous scientific theories associated with

the interaction of human vision and light. But it was not science that put fringe on the lampshade or mermaids on the base. Taste-makers and manufacturers have often been guilty of dressing up or distorting facts in order to push their theories or creations, and the history of popular lighting can be seen as a record of the naiveté and vulnerability of

Painted pot-metal girls are entranced by the glow of a millefiori Czech glass globe. Pot metal (also called white metal or brittania metal) is an alloy of tin with copper, antimony, and sometimes bismuth and zinc. Enhanced by a painted or bronzed finish, it was an affordable substitute for bronze or marble. In the late '20s and '30s it was the preferred material for pop Deco lamps, as ceramic was for 1950s decorative lighting.

the mass market to pseudo-scientific and pseudo-esthetic hype.

Although the English Pre-Raphaelites and American turn-of-the-century Arts-and-Crafts types like Gustav Stickley and the Roycrofters rejected Victorian eclecticism, their preference for natural materials, rural values, and primitive technologies prevented them from embracing the electric lamp as fervently as the urbane, slicker, and more progressive Art Nouveau artisans. Nevertheless, they made lamps and, perhaps more important, urged followers to create their own lighting, giving intellectual justification to the do-it-yourself craze—originally a noble mission—that has given birth to painting by the numbers, home ceramics, the notion that art is therapy, and, obliquely perhaps, the found-object lamp.

When electricity began to penetrate mass-market homes, it is not surprising that mass-market electric lamps began to be produced. Scores of pierced-metal-shade lamps with colored, ribbed, or painted surfaces were patented and produced between 1910 and 1930. Vaguely Art Nouveau, sometimes a bit Crafts-y or Neoclassical, they were always awkward and cheaply produced. Surviving pierced-metal and glass-shade lamps lurk in antique shops awaiting today's version of the uncritical consumer who originally bought them.

By contrast, popular Deco lighting of the twenties and thirties has a considerable following. Somehow pot-metal nymphs tossing a lighted green-glass bubble seem more charming than white-metal slag-glass faux-Tiffanys from Sears. Again, the French (as happened with Art Nouveau) deeply influenced American decorative lighting. Arthur von Frankenberg, inspired by Etling, Le Ver-

rier, and Robj, brought out in the twenties and thirties his own line of night-lights, accent lights, and charming items of decorative illumination—a "premiere" line of mass-market lighting—under the name "Frankart."

Unlike the 1890 to 1910 period, America in the twenties and thirties had no Tiffany or Handel producing true art lamps. Modern lighting was integrated into architecture in the U.S., and some office-y desk lamps were designed by Donald Deskey, Norman Bel Geddes, Walter Von Nesson, and others, but few high-style domestic table lamps were made. Instead, mass-market lamp manufacturers seized the blithe spirit of the French

Moderne style (the "air of questionable levity" Alastair Duncan refers to in *American Art Deco*) and produced legions of graceful girls. These girls were cast in pot metal (not bronze) and accented with molded plastic (not carved ivory). They were a little slurred perhaps and not necessarily elegant, but compared to the tedious home decoration of those who knew better they were exuberant, charming, and indifferent to upper-crust canons of good taste. This folk-Deco spirit incorporated figuralism with a modernistic spin and a love of drama. The spirit lasted from the late twenties on into the 1960s, and it is responsible for most of the lamps in *Turned On.*

Arthur Frankenberg got into the moderne spirit in the '20s, producing lithe pot-metal beauties bearing light for his company, Frankart Inc. This pyramidal metal shade is probably a replacement (although similar shades do show up in Frankart catalogs). Originally inexpensive, Frankart is scarce and pricey today.

July, 1929   LAMP BUYERS' JOURNAL   Fifty-three

Frankart
INCORPORATED

the new line of Lamps will be on view at the Chicago Lamp Show

PALMER HOUSE JULY 8 to 19th.

Frankart
INC.

225 Fifth Avenue
New York

Handbook to Recognized Dealers

No L-228X   U.S Pats. Pend.   Height 11 in.

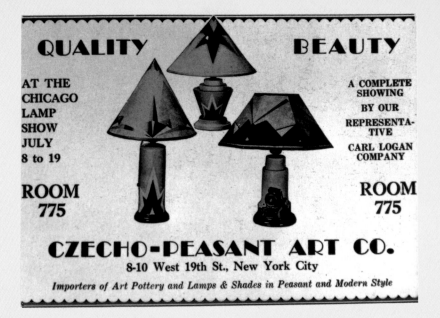

Lamps are a shady affair: a wire frame, some decorated paper or parchment, a few hyperbolic descriptions, and a new industry is born.

All Eyes Turn to **ARTISTIC** *for*
I.E.S. Better Sight Lamps

"Fine appearance . . . low prices"
was promised by makers of '20s
faux-Tiffanys: lamps with shades of
pierced-metal frames backed by
colored, bent glass (sometimes
called "slag" glass).

Another sailing ship for the living room, this one reverse-painted on the glass shade. Bases for these mass-market "art" lamps came in a variety of finishes, all with exotic descriptives such as "rich gilt," "polished brass," "verde Antique," and "statuary bronze." Ah, if saying only made it so.

Traditional lamp styles were adapted to the new technology, as oil and kerosene lamps were wired for electricity.

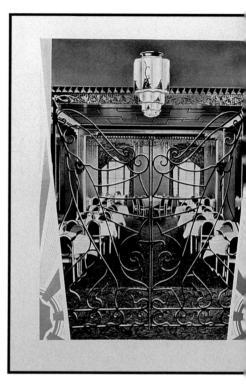

Silhouette lamps of painted metal and frosted glass were often described as "fine for radio cabinets." Like many others, this one is unmarked.

Rembrandt is a name to be
reckoned with, and one way to
appeal to the rising pretentions of
the affluent, postwar American
consumer was to hang the product
on a famous name.

Elegant and simple, this anodized
and brushed aluminum lamp has
been attributed to Kurt Verson. It
still has a paper label "A Genuine
Soundrite Product, Soundrite Corp.,
Holyoke, Mass, U.S.A. Reg. U.S. Pat.
Office."

In the July 1929 issue of *The
Lamp Buyers Journal,* Rembrandt
Lamps Corp. of Chicago presented
the results of its national survey,
which estimated that approximately
$71 million was done annually in
retail lamp and shade trade.

Guys and
DOLLS

Infinitely more interesting as lamp support than an urn or column is the human form. It comes in many shapes and sizes, both venerable and profane, young and old, but mostly it comes as female, and mostly young. From classical Roman times, when Vestal Virgins tended the eternal flame and a perpetual lamp burned in the temple of Venus, women have been the primary keepers of light. They keep the "homefires burning" and the "light in the window." Miss Liberty to this day keeps her torch aloft in New York Harbor. Women were the mainstay of oil lamp support during the Greek, Roman, Renaissance, and Neoclassical periods. For the Victorians, slave girls and goddesses upheld candlesticks and gas lights. Art Nouveau gave new life to the feminine image when lissome, often barebreasted young women in an admirable variety of poses lit our way into the new, electric era.

It is provocative to note that sometime between the pot-metal twenties and thirties and the plaster forties and ceramic fifties, the lamp girls put on clothes. By the fifties, topless was the most a guy could hope for—and then she was not the girl next door but some brown-skinned babe from an exotic land.

The forties and fifties saw the advent of enormous plaster figures, usually in artful pairs (one male, one female) and frequently echoing a thirties motif. With huge shades and ridiculous weight (10 to 15 pounds each), these usually copyrighted "art" lamps would dominate all but the most exuberantly decorated room.

An intriguing subtheme in the outsized-lamp category is the pair with a foreign

Ranch Romance is the theme of this '50s lamp that also tells you what time to tune in *Gunsmoke*. With 24 karat accents, was the West ever more golden?

flavor. One pair we call "The King and I" lamps: Siamese dancers cast in high-glaze ceramic cavort behind Plexiglas columns under pagoda-shaped shades. Seductive third-world women with smiling male companions rhumba and samba in the glow of a three-way bulb.

Occasionally men were the subject of lamp-base sculpture in their own right: a knight in shining armor, a venerable states-man, a stalwart sea captain, a proud laborer, an intrepid hunter. Still, they mostly func-tioned, in the incandescent arena, as com-panion to the female. Lamp design was a world in which the female motif dominated. Interestingly, men ornament clocks more fre-quently than lamps.

The two metal-shade lamps are marked "Geo. I Travio," while the flecked turquoise-and-black chieftain is from "Universal Statuary Co. Chicago, Ill. © 1954." We have also found the Universal mark on a number of oversized plaster pairs of lamps.

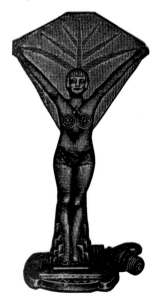

"THE THREE GRACES"

This handsome lamp of two tone art marble is a reproduction of the ever lovely "Three Graces." The figures are beautifully modeled and support a richly decorated 10-inch parchment shade. The shade is bordered at top and bottom with silk ruching and gold lace. The lamp is made in your choice of green or pink decorated, white art marble. Height over all 17 inches. Comes complete with cord and plug. Weighs about 8 pounds packed. Specify color desired when ordering.

2K40024 PRICE complete..................................$9.50

The figure is silver-plated metal and stands on a marble base marked "Fayral."

Painted-metal urns make the bases for this pair of 1930s boudoir lamps. Lamp design was an international business, as evidenced by bases marked "Milwaukee" and shades marked "Germany."

A slender man from the Orient supports a silk-lined wicker shade while a red flamingo hovers near his feet. It is likely that once he had a female companion.

One of the most common TV lamps is this ceramic sampan. The bulb is mounted inside the boat, which is usually found cracked in the center bottom, possibly from the heat of too powerful a bulb.

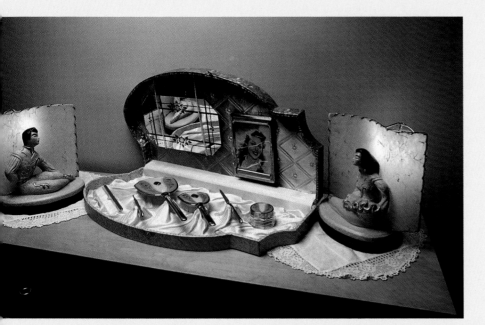

This tall (22½ inches) Oriental man sports a bamboo shade and a characteristically '50s turquoise-colored robe.

Venetian blind shades were popular on '50s lamps; indeed, they create an unusual effect as slices of light stream upward through the slats, and a pool of light illuminates the base.

Massive plaster dancers cavort in couples. The calypso dancers are marked "© 1952 Magidson Bros. Chicago, Ill.," and the other pair are simply marked "Copa." All came with enormous, circular red shades.

She's your Brand X, mythological, dancing javelin-hurler boudoir lamp, who seems equally ready for battle (apparently unaware that her spear is missing) or ballet. No company or individual took credit for this lovely lady.

Lovely ladies as lamp supports are universal; this possibly 1940s dancing girl is marked "J I 520 Italy."

The two-colored harem girl was made by "PGH Statuary Co." of painted plaster.

The crown-shaped paper label still remains: Royal Haeger. Haeger Potteries, Dundee, Illinois, founded in 1871, continues to produce some "artware" and florist-ware today. Royal Arden Hickman designed most of the Royal Haeger line from 1938 to 1944 and was associated with Haeger sporadically until his death in the late 1960s. Despite his lack of formal training, he was considered a folk genius of pottery design, and his TV lamps and decorative-ware are highly sought after by some collectors today.

Pot metal dancers frozen since the 1930s in the raptures of The Carioca.

Oversized lamps with an exotic flavor would have dominated most living rooms. Made of painted plaster they weigh at least ten pounds. Even the finial is oversized and made of the same painted plaster. These are signed "Copa."

Unusual in the world of lighting pairs are these two girls dated 1935. They have slender, moderne physiques in gold-painted plaster.

Possibly inspired by the popularity of *The King and I,* these Far Eastern dancers are set on a Plexiglas stage between black lucite columns and beneath immense, templelike shades.

Animal, Vegetable, or
MINERAL

Play the Twenty Questions Figural and Theme Lamp Game. Pay attention, because we have some electrified beauties that may fit into several categories. Where, for instance, do you put a Mt. Rushmore lamp? Its original owners probably put it atop a late-fifties TV, but we are putting it under "persons"—not "minerals" or "places."

A fair number of these bulb-holding beasts and vegetables were originally sold as TV toppers (we have a whole chapter on that marketing strategy). But since these flora and fauna doubtless migrated from the top of the tube to other rooms and uses, we have not let ourselves get hung up here on their original function.

"Function"?—in the wacky world of popular lighting that's a word that goes together with "form" like horse goes with light bulb. Watts that? Who can avoid being amused at this high-glaze ceramic and plaster zoo? Sure, some are dogs; but there are also roosters, cats, grapes, buffalo, and even a squirrel—or is it a chipmunk? Whatever it is, it's nutty. In the presence of hushed, solemn good taste, these creatures visually bark and squawk and growl.

In each era there were certain preferred motifs and honored subjects. Art Nouveau drew upon the plant kingdom and the sensual curves of women, sometimes combining the two in an early version of biomorphism. These vine-covered lasses seem to have lost ground to the vegetable kingdom. High-style Art Nouveau (especially in Europe but also in the studios of L. C. Tiffany) was filled with lower-order animals—insects, fish, mollusks, bats, spiders, snakes—but they do not seem to have migrated into popular lighting design. Whereas the girls were blithe spirits, very romantic and inaccessible, the animals were cold-blooded, low-slung creatures not generally welcome in the parlors of insurance salesmen and assistant bank managers.

Like much subject matter of '50s figural lamps (the gazelle, panther, greyhound), the fish was a common modernist motif in European '20s and '30s art. This '50s TV lamp has lost all traces of Deco streamlining and exhibits a decidedly '40s surrealistic free-form weightlessness.

An obsession with streamlining in the Deco era brought us lamps in the shape of sleek, exotic creatures like panthers—as well as their fleet prey, gazelles and deer. Domestic speedsters included greyhounds, wolfhounds, and horses. These sinewy, warm-blooded animals were easily translated from high-style Deco to mass-market designs since they have an equally honorable value to all levels of society.

From the pot-metal twenties to the high-glaze ceramic fifties, popular lighting often played upon the themes and echoes of Art Nouveau and Art Moderne, producing inexpensive lighting with charm.

Cut out by hand, this copper elk stands before a frosted-glass moon on a crudely finished board. The Arts and Crafts movement trickles down to the home workshop.

Although not realistic representatives of the animal kingdom, these speeding ceramics exhibit a Deco-esque sleekness and grace.

The spirit of exoticism, which characterized early French Art Deco, was carried on in '50s lamp design as sinewy, low-slung panthers (a preferred animal in both eras) stalked across the Philco or prowled a living-room table.

Exotic princesses with charms to soothe the savage beast.

Our Cocker Spaniel Night Light retains his playful demeanor despite chipped plaster, a frayed cord, and no plug. He sold for $2.95, postpaid, in 1950, but we parted with $10 when he caught our eye in a small antique shop in 1987.

Americans loved all things French in the '50s, and French poodles adorned lamps as well as skirts.

It is likely that this is a '30s lamp, but it was in the '50s that the noble German shepherd returned as Rin Tin Tin to grace our TV screens.

A diligent and determined English setter points up several rare "swamp pheasants."

Not all '50s interiors had orange walls and wire furniture. The pastoral delights of a mythic trouble-free past were evoked by such cheerful lamps as this rooster.

When lamp design takes wing, no type of bird is left un-lamped.

Although insects are uncommon lamp subjects, the beauty of the butterfly did not go unnoticed by lamp designers.

Airbrushed mallards (with and without planters for plastic foliage) were a favorite Mark Trail-y '50s subject.

Ah, the gentle giant (we mean the lamp, not the playful bears climbing it). This weighty plaster beauty lives up to the company's name "Plastart."

After all, it was the Eisenhower era; what more appropriate time for a lumbering elephant lamp?

Only an angler could lust after this leaping fish lamp.

Person, Place, or
THING

Lamps that are out of this world and lamps that *are* this world may be lighting's grandest theme. If a Milky Way or galaxy lamp exists we have not seen it, but Earths that glow from within are popular. And what would a lamp of the universe look like anyway?

Real people are not unknown as subject matter, especially in the era of the pot-metal thirties and forties lamp, when hero worship was more common than today. Personality lamps of the 1950s on are more likely to feature cartoon characters or singing cowboys than politicians or war heroes.

Another theme is transportation—Americans are always on the move, so why not lamps that look as though they may get up and go? Romantic sailing ships are more common than trains or automobiles. Anything of the sea is popular—lighthouses, ships' wheels, mermaids, seashells, lots of fish—but some have washed up in other chapters.

Things of the Old West were fit subject for decorative lighting: horseshoes, cacti, cowboy boots, and wagon wheels. Architectural motifs are often represented, especially if homey subjects like country cottages or hearths or an occasional outdoor barbecue.

All this lamp iconography has dwindled since the fifties. Even the bedroom, once a safe haven for figural boudoir lamps, is now lighted by shaded vases. The rest of the house, too, has been practically swept clean of representational lighting by the Age of Beige's Good Taste Police. Today's echo of figural lamps is found mainly in children's night-lights.

Merchandising popular cartoon characters is a long-established practice. This Mickey Mouse lamp is probably from the late 1940s and is marked "Germany."

In the 1925 *Exposition Internationale des Arts Décoratifs,* a number of lighting devices in the shape of the planet Saturn were exhibited. It took American designers only a short time to turn out their own less costly versions in Depression glass or metal.

These Depression-glass Saturn lamps were also available in blue or white.

By the sea, by the sea, by the beautiful sea, you'll find sailing ships, lighthouses, leaping marlin, and a ship's wheel—and old salts may like to have them in the living room, too.

A Model T-V lamp with some get up and go; horses may have been more abundant, but the ceramic Model T showed up in several colors.

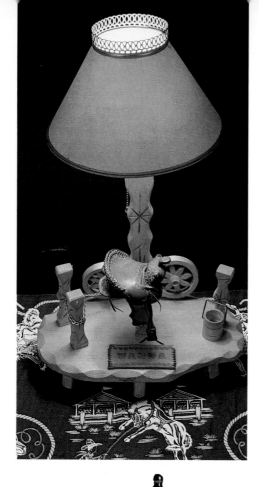

We could not resist a Lamp Named Wanda.

Marked "Maddux of Calif. 8022 A Romane III Rendering © USA of Borglum's Original," this Mount Rushmore is an unusually large piece of ceramic. "Maddux of California," founded in Los Angeles in 1938, was for several decades a highly successful manufacturer of ceramic planters, lamps, figurines, and novelties. Volume fell off in the early '60s as many American manufacturers found themselves unable to compete with low-priced foreign labor, and 1974 was Maddux's last full year.

Davy Crockett, King of the Wild Frontier, had his own television show in the '50s, and "Premco Mfg. Co. Chicago, Ill" presented his fans with Davy and his bear in April 1955.

This sleeping Mexican boudoir lamp probably came as one of a pair. Made of pink Depression glass, including the clip-on shade, it's undoubtedly from the 1930s.

What better way to honor the principles of democracy than by creating a "Spirit of America" novelty lamp, complete with crack in the bell?

Ah, the warmth of hearth and home. Although architectural themes are uncommon in lamp design, they are not unknown. For summer "homefires," we also have an outdoor barbecue grill lamp.

He may not be human, but he is a personality: Charlie the Tuna (© 1970 Starkist Foods) got lucky in the lamp-support game.

One of the less-common souvenirs of the 1933 Century of Progress Exhibition in Chicago was this small, brass lamp made by Chase.

Surrealist Suburban
FANTASIES

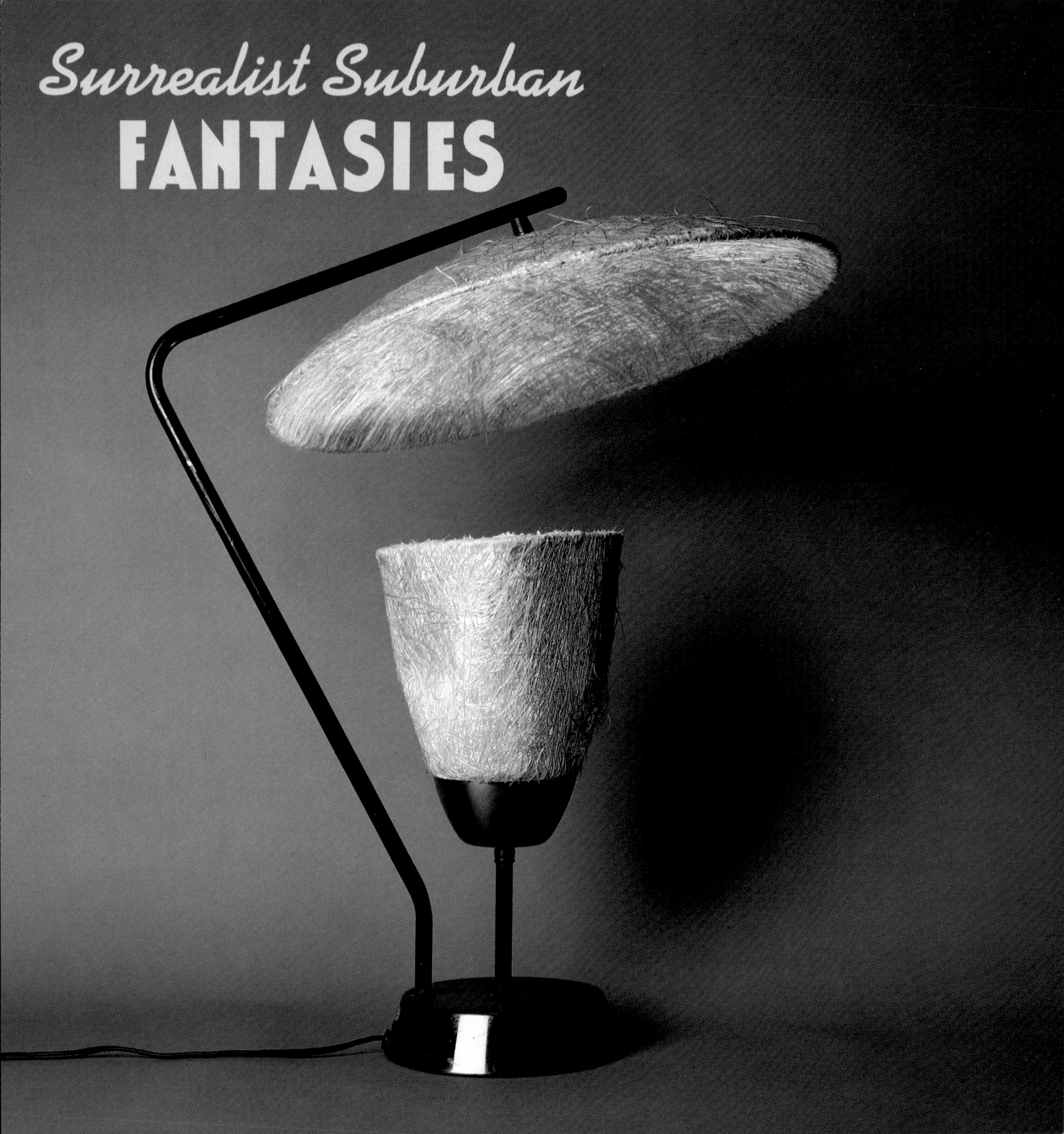

Extremism in support of a light bulb is no vice" might have been the motto of 1950s lamp-designers. Their rear-lit figural ceramic accent or TV lamps, interesting as they are, are clearly French twenties-and-thirties Deco in spirit. The most intensely American fifties lamps seem to grow from the desert after an atomic accident or come from outer space. Often they have integral, free-form shades that are specific to the lamps themselves. They are part of an American radical design style that is destined to be recognized as a pure expression of postwar energy and originality. They can be looked upon as suburban folk-surrealist art lamps.

There is a type of architecture in this postwar period called "Googie." You will recognize it in California coffee-shop roofs that appear to take wing, neon motel signs shaped like boomerangs, and extravagant flashing advertising signs full of color and parabolic curves. Some lamps in this chapter are the portable and collectible equivalent of this rapidly disappearing flamboyant-fifties architectural style. "Googie" lamps.

The word *biomorphic* was often employed in that era. It described a surrealist style that had its origins in biological form, sometimes resembling nature seen through a microscope—or made twisted and grotesque

by bombings. The Atomic Style is a variation on the Futurism theme. When the two concepts met and fell in love, they produced a lamp that was a cross between something picked up on the beach at Big Sur and the Moon Lander.

The war had given us new materials and technologies at affordable costs (fiberglass, plywood, aluminum) and promoted popular recognition of scientific images such as molecular structure, the atomic symbol, sine waves, and amoebic shapes. Bilateral

Lamps with a distinctly science-fiction look arrived with the early atomic-age wave of optimism about technology and departed soon after, as trust in progress was tarnished by fears and anxiety over radiation and pollution. Molecular and atomic decorative motifs were replaced by home designs of a traditional, conservative, and rural nostalgia nature.

Although the shape looks rather like a mushroom cloud from an atom bomb blast, it is probably an evolution of mid-'20s French deco lamps that stacked concentric rings of metal or glass.

ATOM
& Eve

Shell Chemical Company
Chemical Partner of Industry and Agriculture
NEW YORK

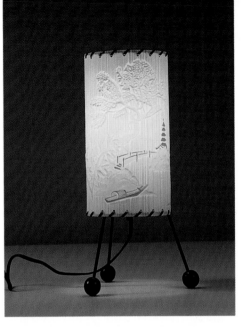

Poised on a slender tripod tipped by "cocktail cherry" feet (borrowed from the molecular model), this lamp has a conventional Oriental scene embossed on its plastic shade. Pop '50s stuff often goes several ways at once.

symmetry, as a design concept, flew (or was thrown) out the living-room window and asymmetry and free form floated back in. These concepts were enthusiastically incorporated into the design of lamps that were and are unlike any other period's lighting fixtures.

Artist's sketch for a magazine ad. The belief in "better living through chemistry," a commercial slogan of the era, was widely held. Such a naive assessment of technology and "the good life" would not survive the era unchallenged.

Atomic motifs saw explosive growth in the postwar era.

Plastic pods burst traditional lamp forms in a postwar lamp that owes more to science fiction than to the history of design. Only the early days of Art Nouveau produced lamps with such color and unfettered imagination.

The amoebic and free-form shapes used in the 1920s and '30s by surrealist artists such as Hans Arp and Joan Miro floated into the suburban home of the 1950s in the guise of tables, sofas, ashtrays, and lamps. The association of such design with the angst of the atomic bomb brought on an antimodernist backlash in the late '60s, banishing until recently home furnishings with a modernist bent.

If nature is the inspiration for this large table lamp, marked "Royal Haeger, Dundee, Illinois," it is not the nature of Planet Earth.

Home furnishings, including lamps, made of bent and welded steel rods looked almost like wry Calder drawings. Originated as a "high style" by designers for Knoll and Herman Miller, this style was quickly adapted, or "knocked off," by mass market distributors.

Although unmarked, this was obviously an expensive, professionally designed lamp. The base is marble and the stems are brass.

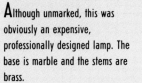

Marked "© F.A.I.P.," this is one of the more tasteful of '50s plaster lamps.

Some '50s lamp styles defy description. It's difficult to imagine the environment they once must have illuminated.

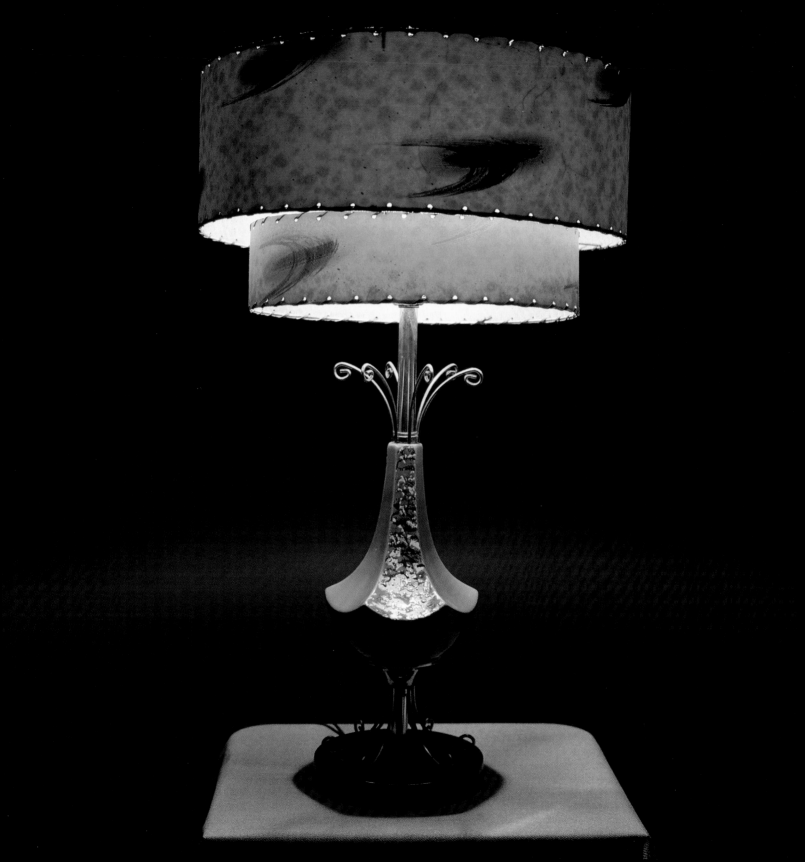

The double (or sometimes triple) shade made of a synthetic material and decorated by splashed or dripped abstract designs is characteristic of many '50s lamps.

Sixty years after the Art Nouveau era, nature could still be a suitable motif for lamps if modernized and abstracted.

Rattan furniture was a favorite of
'30s, '40s, and '50s "smart"
designers. These bamboo lamps with
synthetic shades are perfect with
the late '40s and early '50s
"tropicana" look.

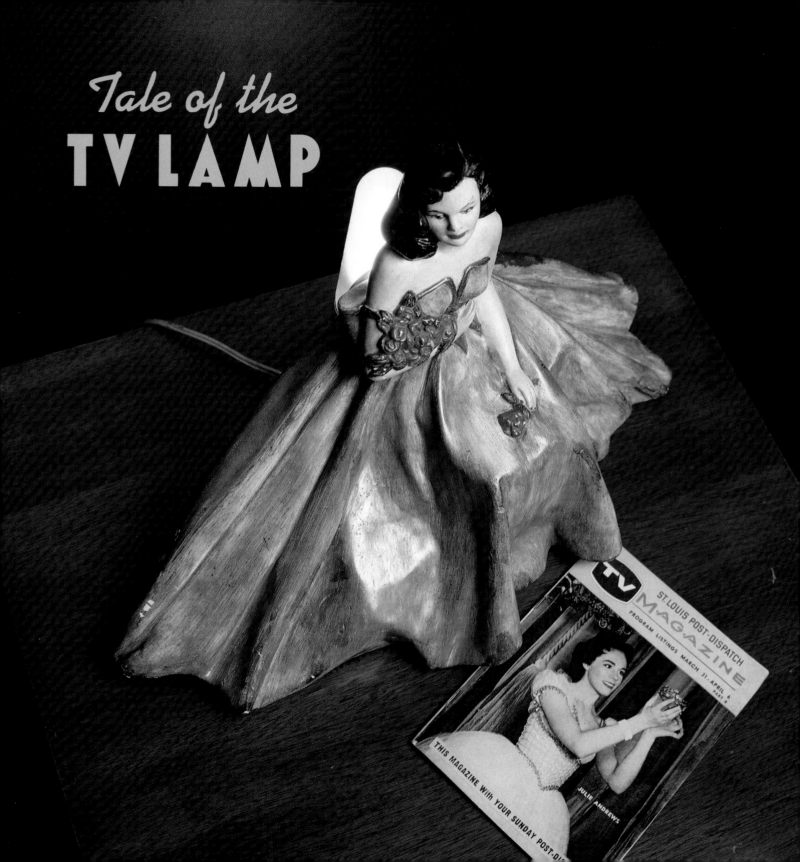

Tale of the TV LAMP

In the early days of television it was thought that one's eyesight would be ruined by watching the TV screen in a darkened room. Some form of indirect lighting near the screen was necessary to ward off eyestrain and eventual retinal damage. In the history of consumer-product development, TV lamps are almost unique in the insane diversity of their solutions to such a simple functional need.

Without this anonymous atomic-age invention, many Baby Boomers might have suffered fusion of the retinal nerves from staring through the inky black into the harsh glare of late-forties and fifties TV screens. But thick glasses and poor visual acuity were acceptable sacrifices for the privilege of worshiping at the tube in those distant, pre-cable, pre-Trinitron days. Without the aid of a slime-green gazelle frozen in a leap above the Philco to bounce a little rod-and-cone-saving light off the wall, the eyeball damage to the Howdy Doody generation would have been catastrophic. In "tasteful" homes without an airbrushed ceramic mallard or chartreuse Chinaman lamp atop the TV, it is rumored that the children often went completely blind. For some, unfortunately, the curtain of night was lowered on their retinas before the eye-endangering black-and-white tube was mercifully replaced by the early color TV, with its slower and less specifically attributable low-level, gene-damaging radiation. There are said to be whole families under institutional care whose big thrill is thumbing through *Reader's Digest* in Braille, all because Mom did not think that a ceramic wolfhound with a light bulb bolted in back belonged in her Ethan Allen living room.

Like many myths of origin the story of the TV lamp's birth is prosaic, and probably this illuminating item was not intentionally fathered at all. More likely it is the offspring of a long-forgotten traveling salesman who seized the opportunity to peddle leftover stock of cheap dime-store backlit radio lamps from the Depression. From this less-than-immacu-

Chanticleer in ceramic. This oversized (13 inches high) "Lane and Co., Van Nuys, Calif. (Pat. applied for)" rooster crows on the Zenith.

late conception the great American public's innate appreciation of function wrapped in artful packaging took over. Initially our nation supported a healthy TV lamp industry, which, in those eyeball-straining days, must have produced over a thousand different forms (we own more than 300 different TV lamps, not counting color variations). Just consider what a service to a whole generation these myriad ceramic beasts provided, which is not to mention their role in acquainting the masses with the dying gasps of the Art Deco style.

With improvements in the video image and larger picture tubes that allowed the spectator to sit back an eye-saving distance, much of the original "function" of the TV lamp was rendered obsolete. Even so its singular esthetic merits remain. We have rescued many important early TV lamps in Good Will stores, junk shops, and flea markets. Covered with grime (inevitably fossil nicotine) and often handicapped by a frayed cord, these exuberant flora and fauna of the golden era of suburbia represent a popular art that has gone extinct in the glacial climate of today's good taste.

The "up light" was a common form during the '30s, very often a floor lamp called a torchiere. There is clearly a deco-esque flair left in the plastic '50s TV lamp.

Although huge numbers of lights were made and sold as TV lamps, hardly any television set advertisements showed a lamp on the console.

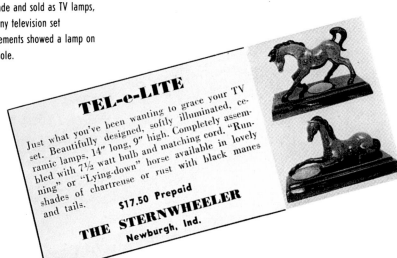

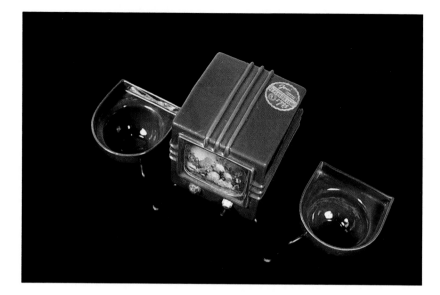

The console television provided a wonderful new surface to decorate. Statuary, vases, planters, pictures of the family, and TV lamps were common ways of dressing up the old tube in its veneered plywood box. This advertisement is unusual in that it shows such an objet d'art on a TV set. The ads of most manufacturers presented unadorned sets in uncharacteristically minimalist interiors.

This wise old TV lamp is signed
"Kron," a lamp designer not a firm.
Kron is also responsible for the
Siamese cats and the poodle and
pug lamps.

The Scottie was the top decorative
dog of the FDR era, a decade or two
earlier than this gilded '50s TV
lamp.

Novelty, boudoir, and radio lamps of the '20s and '30s often used animal motifs like this 1920s glass cat lamp with a pre-Disney Grimmness.

Domesticated felines were a less common lamp subject, but this pair of Siamese cats does show up fairly frequently.

A TV lamp only a cowboy could rope in.

We may have decimated the thundering herds of bison on the plains, but the romance of the Wild West is still embodied in this massive, ceramic buffalo TV lamp. Perfect for a knotty-pine rec room with a maple ranch sofa and wagon-wheel coffee table.

The molded plastic of this classical TV lamp has been scorched by using too big a bulb. Stick to 25 watts or less.

A truly wonderful and rare icon of early television: a glowing Lawrence Welk accordion TV lamp made of translucent ceramic.

Birds are common TV lamp motifs, with ducks, swans, and parrots among the most abundant.

Foliage made a safe statement on the television. This one may be a "realistic" green, but many came exotically airbrushed in multiple tropical colors.

Action and NOVELTY LAMPS

Just when you thought that lamps only sat on a table to brighten your evenings, we bring you action and novelty lamps. They do not just sit there; they do something.

Action lamps combine illumination with some type of interesting movement. As early as the 1920s, revolving Scene-in-Action lamps simulated movement in a pictorial scene on a cylindrical tube surrounding the bulb. Heat rising from the bulb rotated blades at the cylinder's top and moved an interior screen, which was pierced to let light through intermittently. This gave a flickering "action" to the lamp, "endowing beautiful pictures with color, life and movement." Travel to distant places—see gondolas and sampans rocking on moonlit seas, the river plunging over Niagara Falls, Mt. Fuji reflected in rippling waters; survive disaster—see a forest fire rage in your living room, a pirate ship burning. The Aquarium model has a Scene-in-Action pedestal that "enables you to visit the ocean depths," and it supports a two-gallon fishbowl. "Colored light rays, projected from the bulb below, throw myriads of reflected colors on the fish," and undoubtedly keep them warm as well. This lamp form continued on into the 1950s as Hopalong Cassidy and other media heroes "actionned" their way around plastic-topped lamps.

Another kind of mesmerizing, late-Populuxe-era action lamp is the "Shower" light, wherein a plastic figure, usually a semiclothed Venus (or Three Muses) stands classically serene in a plastic garden surrounded by falling raindrops (a clear oil running down monofilament lines). The 1940s pot-metal hula girl stands quiet until the switch is given an extra turn, then her hips begin to sway invitingly.

A cult favorite since its appearance is the lava lamp, which exhibits endless permutations of a bubbling red mass in a golden

Oddly enough, lamps incorporating fishbowls go back to the '20s. If the bulb you use is of too high a wattage, you could end up poaching your goldfish.

The Lava Lite, made by Lava Simplex Corp. of Chicago, has a special nostalgic value to the Baby Boom generation. The soothing, hypnotic vision ("a motion for every emotion") of endlessly undulating globs of wax is now capturing a new and younger crowd.

liquid and was the subject of dreamy fascination in the hippie-dippie sixties. Invented by an Englishman, Craven Walker, about 1964, it was first called the "Astrolight." In 1965 Chicagoans Adolph Wertheimer and Hy Spector bought the exclusive manufacturing and distribution rights for the Americas. They expected it to be a fad, which it was, and to die out in a couple of years, which it did not.

Sales sagged through the seventies, but by the eighties, when the sixties had floated into the netherworld of nostalgia, lava lamps took a leap. They now are to be seen in movies, onstage with rock bands, and in art museums—elevated to their rightful status: "Far Out Icon." Many radio programs celebrating the twentieth anniversary of "Sgt. Pepper's Lonely Heart's Club Band" included lots of "Do you remember when . . . ?" interviews. One now-respectable mother of two recalled first listening to the album while smoking an illegal substance and watching a lava lamp.

The company is now owned by Lawrence Haggerty (once coproprietor of a Fortune 500 company) and is run by his son-in-law, John F. Mundy, a former officer of Penn Central Railroad. It also makes the Confetti Gemlite and the Wave, but neither has achieved the cult status of the Lava Lite. The

newest one, the Midnight Series, is slimmer, comes with tasteful black base and top, and has blue lava. But for the purists among us, only the original, the Century Series, will do.

The novelty lamp comes with a built-in extra-added attraction. And possibly more than one extra feature, function, or decorative element might highlight these dandies. Picture a plaster lamp in the shape of a desk telephone that has a clock in place of a dial, a cigarette lighter in the headset, and is topped by a color-coordinated venetian-blind lampshade. An all-around attractive and useful object by any standard—it is today a true classic of novelty lighting design.

Lamps and clocks are frequently com-

"The Colonial Fountain" lamp was manufactured by the Scene-In-Action Corp. of Chicago in the late '20s. "The graceful fountain continuously spouts a gentle stream of phosphorescent water which as it again descends is transformed into rainbow hues of mist." Made of pot metal with bronze finish, it weighed in at nine pounds.

COLONIAL FOUNTAIN No. 46
Retail Price $6.95

BEAUTIFUL in design and color, the COLONIAL FOUNTAIN'S gentle spray never fails to command intense interest. The graceful fountain continuously spouts a gentle stream of phosphorescent water, which, as it again descends, is transformed into rainbow hues of mist. Surrounding the fountain is a beautiful colonial court backed by stately columns. In the background, huge southern pines rise in splendor against a flawless summer sky. The natural and lifelike color of this scene adds beauty and distinction to any room. Encased in a beautiful lightweight metal frame, finished in bronze. Complete with bulb, switch, silk cord and plug. Weight nine lbs. packed.

JAPANESE TWILIGHT No. 42
Retail Price $6.95

THIS design is one of the most fascinating home lighting effects ever created. Turning on the switch you behold a softly lighted scene depicting the tranquil waters of a hidden lake at the base of Fujiyama in its ageless glory, as seen through the eyes of an artist traveling in the Orient. You see the silver beams of a full Japanese moon reflected by the rippling water. This delightful scene is encased in a beautiful white metal frame of strictly modernistic design, finished in antique silver. Complete with switch, bulb, silk cord and plug. Weight eight lbs. packed.

THE SERENADER No. 44
Retail Price $6.95

THE SERENADER is created from beautifully molded white metal, finished in antique bronze and gracefully set off by a panel of ground-edged glass. It pictures a dreamer's castle in the air, with a pool of glistening water. When lighted, it gives forth a blend of colors never before produced. We call special attention to the fineness in design of metal and glass. If you appreciate statuary bronze, you will want this for the lifelike detail of the base. Rippling moonlight rays, concerted with shifting shadows, create untiring interest. Complete with switch, silk cord and plug. Weight ten lbs. packed.

NOT ILLUSTRATED

No. 47   Marine Model $4.95
No. 45   Moonlight Model 4.95

Printed in U.S.A.

FOREST FIRE No. 41
Retail Price $4.95

THE FOREST FIRE design is so realistic in color and action that you will hardly believe your eyes. You see a dense northern forest, stately pines, a hunter's cabin, a raging fire traveling at a terrific rate of speed, apparently destroying everything in its path, black smoke clouds rolling skyward, the cabin rapidly taking flame and the massive trees slowly succumbing to the intense heat. All this you actually see in action. It is a sight you will never forget, and a lamp you will want to own. Complete with incense burner, bulb, silk cord and plug. Weight, five lbs. packed.

SCENE-IN-ACTION
DISTINCTIVE, UNIQUE, APPEALING, DECORATIVE

SCENE-IN-ACTION creations are distinctive, unique, appealing, decorative — the latest contribution to artistry in lighting. They brighten that dark nook, improve and beautify the room, and decorate the mantel. The softly colored rays make them particularly adaptable for use as night lights. The small bulb permits their constant use, day and night. Designs No. 41, No. 43, No. 45 and No. 47 are equipped with perfume burners of unusual effectiveness. A few drops of your favorite perfume, with an equal quantity of water will rapidly permeate an entire house. SCENE-IN-ACTION products operate on either AC or DC current.

A RICH ORNAMENT FOR ANY ROOM

AQUARIUM No. 50
Retail Price $7.95

DISTINGUISHED from all other forms of animated lighting effects, the above aquarium must be seen to be appreciated. The metal base is beautifully finished. The pedestal, equipped with SCENE-IN-ACTION, enables you to visit the ocean depths. You see submarine life in its natural state — mammoth fish swimming about, ocean currents briskly churning the sandy bottom, and every natural color brought out to its best advantage. The two-gallon bowl on the pedestal has a transparent crystal rock in its bottom. Colored light rays, projected from the bulb below, throw myriads of reflected colors on the fish. Equipped with bulb, switch, silk cord and plug. Size 12"x14". Weight, nineteen lbs. packed.

SCENE-IN-ACTION
GUARANTEED QUALITY IN EVERY LAMP

All SCENE-IN-ACTION products are manufactured of the highest grade non-inflammable materials obtainable. They are offered for sale only after SCENE-IN-ACTION engineers have completed exhaustive tests. Every one is assembled, thoroughly inspected and tested for defects before it is packed. The Scene-in-action Corporation guarantees all of its products to be free of defective materials or workmanship.

bined with great effect. We can (sort of) understand a clock set in the center of a decorated-vase lamp base, but to put one under the hooves of a proud black stallion? A particularly lovely combination lamp is a lighted disk with a clock in the center surrounded by an underwater scene with two angel fish "swimming" around the clock.

There is as well the "comment" lamp like the ceramic drunk leaning on a lamppost with a glowing red bulb for a nose. One can choose from an almost endless list of sports-theme lamps for gift giving: golf, tennis, bowling, baseball, football, and fishing. The spirit of Art Nouveau truly lives in a cluster of plastic grapes that glow from within.

The companies may change, but the Scene-in-Action style continues: a speeding locomotive, a '60s Op Art lamp, and the Hopalong Cassidy Animated Action lamp advertised in *House Beautiful,* August 1950. Really good ideas never die.

The Shower-Lite is manufactured by Creators Lamp Co. of Chicago and is available as either a swag lamp or a table lamp. Most of us are familiar with the classical lady (Diana, Venus, Water Lady, or Dancer) standing amid the plastic greenery, but few have realized that an Old Country Mill with functioning water wheel is available.

ART MARBLE LAMP

This lamp, which stands about 12½ in. high, is an amazing value, for here you have an artistic piece of art marble sculpture. The lamp is complete with shade, silk cord and plug. A clock with American made movement adorns the center. The base is white art marble, relieved with a touch of green. The shade is parchment, decorated and edged. The clock has a gilt bevel and silvered dial. It is hard to believe such an amazing combination can be offered at such a small price.

2K25155 PRICE.....................$7.75

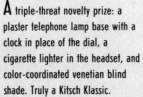

A triple-threat novelty prize: a plaster telephone lamp base with a clock in place of the dial, a cigarette lighter in the headset, and color-coordinated venetian blind shade. Truly a Kitsch Klassic.

An early home-entertainment center: this '40s wood-veneer table lamp houses a Telechron clock and an AM Philco radio in its base.

Drunks leaning on lamp posts must have lit many a rec room. Several types have light-up noses as well as light-up street lights.

A '50s descendant of the early 20th-century "husk" lamps: here tiny, colored bulbs are the pistils of the flowers in the wire basket.

Italy is home to this glowing plastic caveman.

The Mackey Manufacturing Co. of Chicago called this glowing paperweight a "Gazing Globe." Some of these came with a languorous nude lounging beside the light. A late-'20s novelty lamp, it has a surprisingly heavy base (possibly plaster) that came in either a copper or green finish.

Our pot metal Pablo is probably from the '30s. He came originally with a round, frosted bulb that had a mustachioed face painted on it. There is also a cowboy version.

A large ceramic monkey sports a manic grin, waiting for you to drop a few coins in. Marked "© C. Miller," this is the only bank–lamp combination we have seen.

Incorporating a light source into an existing object is not a new idea. Mollusk shells have served the ancients as ready-made oil lamps, and, less commonly, human skulls have been used to support candles. But these are timid and unimaginative when compared to the creations of American do-it-yourselfers. A blowtorch, a parking meter, a wagon-wheel hub, a Buick transmission (ca. 1935), a real coal stove (the heaviest lamp we have seen)—these are a few of our favorite found-object lamps. This is not to demean those made with Clorox bottles, washing-machine agitators, coffee grinders, seashells, Popsicle sticks, and other more pedestrian articles of daily life.

Not all of the raw material for found-object lamps can be considered junk. Professionals have turned people's treasured mementoes into lamps for years. *Lighting and Lamp Design* by Warren E. Cox, published in 1952, chronicles years of converting everything from Ming vases and eighteenth-century porcelains into lamps and creating shades from such leftovers as "one of 18 prints . . . from William Blake's original copper plate etchings of Chaucer's Canterbury Pilgrims. . . ." Similar lamps were commercially manufactured, probably in small workshops, using such diverse materials as seashells, cannon shells, cholla cactus, and even (ugh) deer feet. (Or should we have categorized the latter under "animal"? As you can see, the taxonomy of lamp design is no laughing matter.)

The restless need to turn the detritus of modern life into something "useful" has multiple roots. The Victorians had a love of crafts that left us with shadow boxes filled with art-

The High Kitsch triumvirate of Found Object lamps: a parking meter (yes, you have to feed the meter to keep the light on), a fire extinguisher with part of a cream separator for a shade, and a carpenter's plane with a wooden beer spigot to support the socket. It doesn't get much better than these.

Lighten your load on laundry day with this washing-machine-agitator lamp. To add sparkle to chore-time, this special base has been painted gold. In the unlikely event that a 2,000 watt bulb might someday be needed, the creator also salvaged the extra-heavy-duty washing-machine electrical cord.

fully arranged mementoes such as locks of hair, feathers, photos, fans, shells, and "memory" bottles covered with bits of broken pottery, pieces of jewelry, buttons, and charms. Another energizing force behind the do-it-yourselfers was the Arts and Crafts movement, whose antimachine sentiment glorified *anything* made by the human hand.

Once the need for a lamp's oil reservoir was past, the imaginations of lamp-designers and do-it-yourselfers alike were set free. Unlike instruments of necessary functionalilty and classic beauty (the hammer, the sailing ship, the microscope) the electric lamp is as liberated from design restraint as anything can be, save a blank canvas. Even better than the canvas, it is self-illuminating. The form can be anything, taken from anywhere—and frequently is.

Ponder as well the "found shapes" left over from earlier technologies. No small number of these are actual lighting objects that have been wired for electricity, such as candlesticks and oil and gas lamps. Even

more abundant are lamps with an archaic lighting theme, harking back to pre-electric days. Ho-hum . . . we'd rather sit in the dark. It took a greater spirit of adventure to make a table lamp out of a World War I artillery shell with machine-gun bullet pulls than it did to run a wire through Grandma's brass candlestick.

Mixed messages come through in the photo-transfer shade that shows peacefully grazing animals on a lamp made of the appendages of a three-footed deer.

"The Anything Lamp Kit" offered a method of incorporating a vase or statue into a lamp base without damaging the "objet d'art" in the process.

The joys of recycling are apparent in this lamp base made from 1930s cigarette packages.

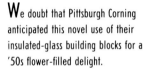

Items of significance, rendered obsolete by technological change, often find their way into lamp bases. A pay telephone lamp was among the choice Americana offered at a Bouckville, New York, antique market.

We doubt that Pittsburgh Corning anticipated this novel use of their insulated-glass building blocks for a '50s flower-filled delight.

In this case the lamp base is a "found person." (Cartoon by George Wolfe, reprinted from *The Saturday Evening Post,* © 1943 The Curtis Publishing Co.)

Wars leave a lot of spent and surplus artillery shells. Do-it-yourselfers find these brass cylinders inspirational lamp bases. Caution: Be *sure* the shell is not full of gunpowder before drilling it.

"Did I tell you—Junior has been studying camouflage lately also."

For a truly tropical flavor, how about a cayman night light? Be careful changing that bulb!

House Beautiful (November, 1964). The homes featured in the magazine rarely if ever contained such "Marvels of Nature" as these cypress-knee lamps advertised in its back pages. Souvenirs of the Florida swamps, they were manufactured in Michigan.

Mementoes from the sea have a long history as souvenir-ware. Conch shells from the Gulf of Mexico are frequently found in the 2,000-year-old midden heaps of Ohio Indians. Shell and plaster lamps acquired on a 1950s Gulf Coast vacation are not unknown in the garage sales of suburbia.

The Quest for
ENLIGHTENMENT

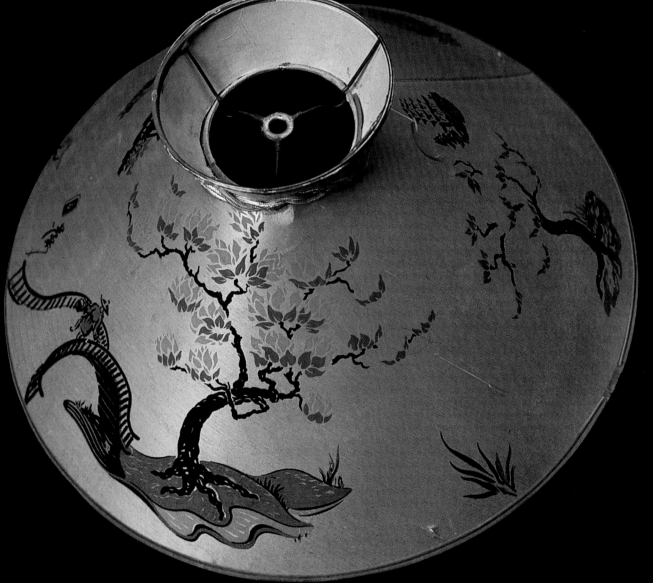

The fate of unstylish plug-in bulb holders, i.e. lamps, is melancholy. Once the shining pride of a happy household, they are all too often cast out with years of service still remaining. Homeless and likely as not divorced from their original shades, they accumulate in dreary secondhand stores and Good Wills. Even though the majority are insipid variations on the drilled vase or ornamental urn theme, now and then a comely specimen can be found even in the lowliest habitats.

Folk Deco or fifties-naive modern lamps are quickly grabbed up from junk stores and reappear married to period shades in Deco shops. At the time of this writing (early 1989) TV lamps are mostly $30 to $75 retail, with the more desirable ones going from $125 up to $175. Decent fifties table lamps can be had for under $75, but the really extreme jobs with designed shades are several hundred and up. Prices are now a little higher in California than on the East Coast. Most of the lamps in this book cost us under $50, and we collected them from New York to L.A. Fortunately, not everyone holds in high esteem lamps in the form of hula girls and poodle dogs.

Always check the wiring before turning on—old lamps can be shocking in more ways than one! Lamp repair is a major craftsy pastime, so the public library has plenty of books on rewiring electric lamps. If you are not handy with tools, small-appliance repair shops or some lamp stores will replace frayed cords for a reasonable charge. Bad cords can cause shorts or fires no matter whether the fixture is turned on—if it is plugged in.

If at all possible, turn the lamp on before buying. The personality of a lamp changes dramatically when the light comes on. Lamps that may look dead in the dark leap to life as the rays stream down. Some

Generations of small lamp-and-shade makers have produced lighting fixtures in every conceivable mixture of styles. Vintage shades such as this vaguely Chinese design from the 1930s are frequently found in second-hand stores or antique shops.

The one that got away! I turned to take a picture at the Brimfield, Massachusetts, antique market, and someone bought this wild little lamp before I could. The period of most extreme '50s style only lasted about 10 years (1954–1964), and already there is keen competition for the best examples.

lamps that look great unlighted wilt under incandescent glare. Problems of pitted pot-metal finishes and chips, cracks, and dings are also illuminated.

Shades, too, experience metamorphosis with the addition of light. How they handle the glow can completely alter their look. Many lamps were sold without shades, allowing the purchaser to exercise her creativity in combining lamp, shade, and living room. Shades, easily damaged, were the first part to be replaced, re-covered, or discarded, so good period shades can be hard to find. For high-glaze ceramic lovelies from the fifties, a good match is often a circular double shade with the characteristic drips and squiggles on a cream background. Do not pass up a truly outrageous lamp for lack of a shade—and vice versa. If you are willing to haunt the markets you can sometimes make a surprising match.

Consider carefully the bulb you use.

After all, you worked up the nerve to buy the lamp and take it home. Do not clutch up now. This is your chance to let yourself go: bulbs come in many shapes, colors, and wattages. Maybe that lovely white-and-gold baby would sparkle with a red light. Do not use over 25 watts in TV lamps unless you want them to self-destruct, but they too can benefit from color. There are bulbs that flicker like candles, long skinny bulbs, and clear bulbs that show the glowing filament. Whatever you choose, be sure the lamp's wiring is up to it.

And how does one illuminate one's domicile with such works? You will get no advice from period shelter and decorating magazines. The best lamps, which is to say the worst (according to the Good Taste Police), are conspicuous in their absence from the colorful feature articles and professional decorator "Tips" columns. We have

In their own time the authorities on "good" taste were repelled by the more daring '50s designs. Even relatively modest '50s lamps such as these scarcely show up in the numerous books on '50s interior decoration.

Faux Nouveau and fake Tiffanys from the teens and '20s are often pricey. Their tags of $300 to $800 reflect the popular nostalgia for anything with an archaic air. Will the baby boomers similarly value the stuff from their childhoods? Check your aunt's attic for the black panther TV lamp, the one with the glowing ruby eyes.

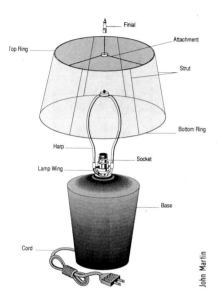

Finial
Attachment
Top Ring
Strut
Bottom Ring
Harp
Socket
Lamp Wing
Base
Cord

John Martin

A few lamps from an earlier, more exuberant suburbia can lighten up even the tedious blandness of today's tract-house interiors.

collected hundreds of pages of ads for fifties TVs, and not a single one sports a figural TV lamp. The "take me to your leader" type of fifties table lamp is unknown in the featured interiors of *House Beautiful.* Occasionally, in the back of the magazine, in little black-and-white ads, small manufacturers will offer a funky lamp by mail order—but that is the exception.

　　You are on your own as to how to decorate with them. They are strong enough not to be intimidated by large expressionist paintings or Mexican masks, if that is of any help. They are compatible with Postmodern interiors and brightly colored furniture of a nontraditional nature, too. We cannot say how they work with chintz and damask or rocking horses and ruffled curtains. Teddy bears are, after all, the preferred prey of back-lit, high-glaze black panthers.

Kitschy and corny '50s lamps are easier to find than abstract examples. The Annex, a Sunday outdoor market on 6th Avenue in New York City, is a good place to find '50s design of all kinds, as is the thrice yearly Brimfield, Massachusetts, outdoor market.

We would like to give special thanks to Walton Rawls, a truly enlightened editor, and to Julie Rauer, of Abbeville, who designed the book. To John Margolies, whose work we admired long before we met him, our thanks for his support and enthusiasm. To friends and family whose support and enthusiasm have been constant, especially Homer C. Wadsworth, Mrs. Alleen P. Johnson, Dale Eldred, Ralph T. Coe, Jeremy Adamson of the Renwick Gallery, and Sam Pennington of the *Maine Antique Digest.*

Many dealers and collectors across the country were generous with their collections: Mary Lou Janssen, Sedalia Antiques, Sedalia, Missouri; Virginia Teel Chace of the Viking Flea Market, Springfield, Missouri; Mike Cochran and Randy Ebrite of Nellie Dunn's, Springfield, Missouri; Perry's General Store, Springfield, Missouri; Carol Rittit, manager of the Art Deco Show in Indianapolis; Barbara Strand and Daniel Toepfer of The Good, the Bad, and the Ugly, New York City; June Varney, Springfield, Missouri; Duane Crigger, Springfield, Missouri; Stan Guffey and Frank Ward of High Brow, Nashville, Tennessee; Roger Ellingsworth, Royal Oak, Michigan; Carrie Homann, Champaign, Illinois; Linda Katz and Laura Misenick, Cleveland, Ohio; Janet Phillips of Feathers, Dayton, Ohio; Kevin Cooper, Indianapolis; Marty and Nancy Manly, Beech Grove, Indiana; Doug Ramsey, Birmingham, Michigan; Bobbi Owens, Miamitown, Ohio; Pam Mangan of Blue Sun Gallery, Indianapolis; Donna Gibson, Evansville, Indiana; Doris Aberson, Indianapolis; Charles Alexander, Indianapolis; Paul Harris, Indianapolis; and Andy Lopez of The Plastic Arts of Jackson, Michigan.

Lava Simplex Internationale, Chicago, Illinois, generously shared the complete history of the Lava Lite with us.

And our thanks go also to the 250 watt illuminators of popular culture: Edward Lucie-Smith, Bevis Hillier, Thomas Hine, Robert Venturi, Denise Scott-Brown, and Steven Izenour, whose work has helped shape and refine our perceptions.

Finally, a deep bow to the dynamo of democratic esthetic theory, Thorstein Veblen, more current today than ever before.

The ideas for this book (and most of the lamps) came from our experiences in outdoor flea markets, the trenches of the antiques trade. Our thanks to the dealers, collectors, and promoters from coast to coast who have helped shape our perceptions. This fraternity of entrepreneurs is a floating avant-garde of trends and directions often years ahead of museum shows and slick magazine articles.